Spitting Back!

Bruce O'Brien

Table of Contents

Copyright

For John: Promise made. Promise kept.

INTRODUCTION

For over 150 years, the left and their sycophants in education, media, Hollywood, and their dominance of culture have been spitting in my face. Now, I have a remarkable individual in the White House, and together, we are—Spitting Back!

Since 1848, my enemies have led a ruthless assault on me: my principles, my beauty, my wisdom, and the idea that I love them more than they hate me. All of this baffles them. The shallowness of their totalitarian aspirations is glaring to those of us who open our eyes. The goal of this book is not to convince but to assist in the eye-opening experience. It is to encourage both young and old to seek the opinions of those who lie outside the left's cultural hegemony and then engage.

Who am I? I am the common woman and man. I am the backbone of humanity. I am the lover of Western civilization and its bold commitment to the truth, the steady progressive advancement of humanity, and its fight for justice. The commitment to the empathy of the West (thank you, Helen) is demonstrable through me by my obvious historical love of my fellow woman and man. I have been trifled with for far too long.

It is indeed unfortunate that this point of our cultural development has forced me to take the gloves off. I will no longer be intimidated by the self-anointed "experts" flaunting their degrees in nonsense and forcing me to adhere.

I am not Bruce O'Brien. I am the common woman and man. And… I am Spitting Back!

Let us continue.

CRITICAL RACE THEORY

SUCKS

Using the ubiquitous negativity of Critical Theory, which has saturated the intolerant elite, Critical Race Theory exploits the dark side of humanity to crush the remarkable anthropological success of Western civilization. It applies the ugly violence of Marxist methodology (by any means necessary) with the attraction of shallow conspiracy (Derrick Bell's Interest-Convergence Thesis) to actually come up with the biggest conspiracy theory in human history. Whether looking at the original concept of critical theory through Max Horkheimer of the Frankfurt School or the evolved contemporary Cultural Marxist version, of which CRT is today's calendar girl for critical theory, the results are the same: hate, violence, and, quite possibly, in the case of CRT, White genocide.

Under a constant barrage of negativity, which sustains critical theory, the default position of human nature is bad behavior. This is inevitable and by design; to move toward the perverted concept that the only path to human progress is protracted bad behavior. In other words, steady and increasingly more violent revolution. The harbingers of genocide are all in place: propaganda, dehumanization, demonization, racism, intolerance, speech suppression, systemic indoctrination, flagrant lying, violence messaging, eliminationism. Adolf and Mao would be proud. If I may quote the brilliant Dr. James Lindsay, "If Critical Race Theory ever reaches its logical conclusion, that logical conclusion is White genocide." Well said. As Dr. Lindsay observes, what we are witnessing in today's nasty racism against Whites is a mirror image of Mao's cultural war against the "intellectual bourgeois" of China, and, I will submit, Hitler's cultural war against the Jews. Only the Left could foist the evils of bigotry and racism onto our kids and then have the balls to call it social justice.

The creation of critical theory, which is now ubiquitous throughout every classroom in America, is an outgrowth of the failure of "Vulgar Marxism" (the disparaging back-room reference to the failed materialist aspect of communism by the Frankfurt scholars themselves). It is astounding how the far left can be repetitively proven wrong and yet consistently rebound with another crock of shit, and then shoehorn it into the indoctrinating universities. Since 1848, has it never occurred to them that, given a choice, people would rather do what is best for themselves and their neighbors than for the elites? I think it has, and… they don't care.

This is not going to stop. And, according to the famously intellectually vacuous nitwit, Kamala Harris, in her praise for BLM violence, it should not. One could not expect more from a drunk. However, if we do expect more—much more—from the equally vacuous intelligentsia who line up for their degrees, we will always be disappointed. To quote the inimitable Thomas Sowell, "The road to hell is paved with ivy league degrees."

The left has consistently supported the genocidal monsters of the 20th century: Lenin, Stalin, Mussolini, Hitler, Mao, Pol Pot, and their sycophants. Critical Race Theory is their latest three-wheeled vehicle to human catastrophe. They know it, and they like it.

WHAT IS WOKE?

At first, to me, that seems like a stupid question. But when I step back and think about it, that is because I'm old and can easily identify the linguistic nuances that have gradually saturated our shared languages, and from that, I can identify the creeping tentacles of woke. Linguistic manipulation as a tool of deception has been perfected by the left.

From the ashes of World War II, "Never Again" was a cultural battle cry that was fully understood. Do millennials and Gen Z understand the visceral reaction of boomers when they hear that phrase? I don't think so. Have they even heard that phrase? And if they have, do they care? Or is it just… antiquated sloganeering? Have you been to a university campus, any university campus, in the last 10 years?

I'm sure that some will take offense at the implications of that paragraph, and that is good. But others will understand the point, and that is good because it underlines what I'm saying, which is: Antonio Gramsci's "Long March through the Institutions" has come to fruition, setting the stage for "Never Again" to happen again. Even Tony, arguably a Fabian Marxist, could never have seen woke stealing his totalitarian plan.

The repetitive arguments back and forth over what is woke, not woke, kinda woke, maybe woke—depends on who you ask—that is woke, this is not, yadda, yadda, blah, blah, blah—are wasting valuable time. *That is by design,* as one of the methodological exercises of Totalitarian Cultural Marxism, of which woke is the driving force, is to sow as much confusion as possible (illegal immigration, pronouns, gender ideology, Jews suck, Critical Race Theory, white people suck, etc.) to further erode societal cohesion. This is crucial to the destabilization required to topple society first and then establish totalitarianism. And yes, totalitarianism can be repeatedly found throughout the history of Marxist literature— from Marx to the Frankfurt School, to Mao to Woke. It's all there, in plain sight.

So, Dear Reader, please allow me to give you a traditional three-phase definition in the interest of brevity so we can move on to address the serious consequences of this insidious and downright evil ideology without wasting our valuable time.

Woke *n.*

1. The cultural destruction of Western civilization to pave the road to totalitarian Cultural Marxism.

2. The process of implementing the political concept of Totalitarian Cultural Marxism while masquerading as diversity, equity, and inclusion by utilizing an indoctrinating methodology to establish unquestionable praxis. This is achieved through subversive domination of education.

3. They're coming for your kids.

There you go. That's it. Now, let's get to work and expose this monstrosity before it's too late. Before the "Never Again" of the 20th century happens again.

BLM AND THE KLAN

Both are one and the same.

KKK: Racist White Supremacists.

BLM: Racist Totalitarian Marxists.

Both are (were?) violent hate-mongers residing comfortably within the matrix of Violent Conflict Theory. Neither of these abhorrent organizations' ideologies should be allowed in our education system, especially K-12. Yet, BLM has a huge presence there, but the Klan, thank God, does not. The Klan is, for all practical purposes, obsolete. Had it been born in the 21st century, it never would have seen the least success, and its leaders would be in jail. That is because this beautiful country took seriously the teachings of Dr. King. BLM, however, despite having been exposed for the absolutely fraudulent, hate-filled, and stunningly corrupt organization that it is, hang gliders and all, is not only still around and *rejecting* Dr. King, but still allowed in our schools. The Klan were murderous thugs. BLM was, and I will argue, still are, murderous thugs. Marching for BLM is marching for the Klan—just a different colour.

So, what's up? Cultural Marxism... that's what. The wave of cultural Marxism and its goal of crushing Western Civilization (caps intended) needs the likes of Antifa and BLM to do its dirty work, and there is no better way than to aid and abet hordes of know-nothing, nitwit activists who have no idea what they are doing. "Burn it all down" and "By any means necessary" are the age-old Marxist tropes they are screaming in the streets. And why wouldn't they? They are being used by the know-nothing, nitwit universities. The "mostly peaceful" virtue-signaling protesters are in common cause with BLM and the universities and, by extension, lighting their Molotov cocktails. These mindless robots are engaging in criminal behavior thinking it is "social justice" as they support the Jew-hatred and vile anti-white hillbilly racism of BLM and the ivy league.

They should all be in jail, and in a non-totalitarian society, they would be. They should be sharing cells with the Klan-supporting white supremacists. Those logistics should not be a problem, seeing as both of these disgusting organizations have been, and still are, completely populated by democrats. With only a sliver of cognitive ability, they should get along just fine.

The contemporary argument from the right is that democrats are racist against White people. While true, this is not how the racists always find their way to the Democrat Party. The reason the Democrat Party is *always* the party of racists (and anti-Semites) is political opportunism. In the 20th century, anti-black racism found its political home in the Democrat Party. In the 21st century, anti-white racism finds its political home in the Democrat Party. It is not, in essence, that the democrats are *necessarily* racist. It is that they are, first and foremost, hate-mongering, politically opportunistic twits. They live on hate and violence, whether it is in their hearts or the hearts of others, and will manipulate it for political power. Hate is not merely another tool in the toolbox for achieving totalitarian power. It is the toolbox.

Burn it all down… by any means necessary.

HUMAN NATURE

Human nature is the most important consideration in all fields of intellectual endeavor, from Aristotle to Newton to Freud to Peterson. (Yes, Peterson.) Yet the left treats it like a joke. This is what embracing postmodernism will do to an otherwise productive mind. The attraction of postmodernism to young wannabe scholars is the pleonastic vocabularies of the likes of Judith Butler and Michel Foucault, who dazzle them with nonsense but are basically saying this: Let's not work; let's get drunk; let's stay drunk; let's rape kids; and give each other blow jobs. That's it. Pretty basic stuff.

My (shared?) thesis on PM is that it never evolved on an intellectual plane of its own. It has evolved from Freud with a large dose of Marx and his ridiculous concept of altering the human mind to achieve societal utopia. Add in Foucault, looking to excuse his hedonistic lifestyle through intellectual bullying, and bingo—there it is! Postmodernism! A primordial soup of irresponsible lunacy coming to a university near you! Great.

Marx was intellectually more formidable than the postmodernists who followed him, though he was, especially for his time, just as dangerous. For all his brilliance, he simply would not accept that human nature does not allow for perfection. No amount of indoctrinating social engineering will ever change the being of woman and man.

The Marxist/Maoist-Freirian/Marcusian methodology of molding the human mind from birth to create a politically totalitarian utopia is a recipe for genocide. The human brain is psychiatrically hard-wired. Psychologically, it is not. So, by psychologically manipulating the mind, when the shit hits the fan, it will always default to its psychiatric position. Think of it as the hard drive and the complementary software. (Actually, with what we now know about DNA communication, that is exactly what it is, but that will have to be another discussion at Billerica U.)

Collectivism, as it has been for all species, was psychiatrically hardwired for survival purposes long before the "Cognitive Revolution." Since the CR, capitalism gradually evolved as woman and man developed in a deterministic way to seek comfort. It was not created by woman and man, but slowly became psychiatrically hardwired into their being (through updates?). Marxist theory, extrapolated from collectivism, *was* created by man and, therefore, is psychological. The inevitable clash of varying psychological positions under Marxist/communist/socialism sets up humankind for failure. Once it fails, which it always has and will, it will default to capitalism because capitalism works—naturally. Unfortunately, the completion of this cycle is never achieved without the slaughter of a significant portion of the population.

The woke left doesn't know, care, or both.

THE FAIRNESS CONUNDRUM

An open mind reserves the right to change when enough empirical and logical information demonstrates the necessity for that change. A problem arises, however, when the source presenting the evidence is not open-minded. If it is an ideologically captured source that is devoted to your total destruction, "by any means necessary," then your open-minded acquiescence becomes another notch in his diabolical belt.

This is why I maintain that any vote for any democrat, whether you agree or not, anywhere on the ballot, from president down to dog catcher, strengthens the Marxist obsession with the obliteration of Western civilization and emboldens the culture of violence ensconced in the Democrat Party. The absolutism of violent cultural Marxism in the American Democrat Party makes them the most dangerous political party in the world.

To quote Thomas Sowell (who, like Nietzsche, "… could say more in one sentence than most scholars can say in a book"): "Democrats are the only reason to vote for republicans." Indeed. Especially if you want to live in peace.

Unfortunately, we have reached the point where cooperative collusion leading to progressive compromise, which is the essence of democracy and the heart of Western civilization, is no longer available. If you give an inch, they will crush you. The survival of the most progressive, most beautiful, and inclusive civilization humankind has ever known is under rapacious attack. There is no compromise. There is no fairness. There is only one solution.

Stop voting for democrats.

GRASPING AT STRAWS

Real Marxism had failed. The Frankfurt School understood this, and so they had to come up with something (and fast) to feed their psychopathic, narcissistic, and intellectually blind hatred of capitalism and classical liberalism. They were grasping at straws. A real man would have just admitted he was wrong.

It has always fascinated me how the musings of a handful of the "Great Thinkers" of humanity could be so directly responsible for historical atrocities, yet those "thinkers" never bear the consequences. Anyway…

How do they manage this dance through civilization? The Universities. They are well-fed by the doting left-wing administrators who have taken quite seriously Antonio Gramsci's "Long March Through the Institutions" (Dutschke quote), and the monsters of postmodernism. While conservatives dismissed them all as insignificant quacks, they were oblivious to their own hubris. The "quack" part was spot on. The "insignificant" part was a deadly mistake.

Well-disciplined, intolerant, and devoted to Marx's irrational utopian cause, these academics concentrated their efforts on young, vulnerable minds, knowing they would take their cause through the institutions of civil society to make them as non-civil as possible. Hate and violence are celebrated as hallmarks in their twisted ideology and "necessary means" of achieving the greater good. The Soviet defector, Yuri Bezmenov, explained that the Soviets understood that once ideological capture was programmed into students, they would carry it through their lives, and the only way to stop it would be to deprogram. (This explains intelligent people being excited by a moron like Kamala Harris.) By the time the opposition (conservatives) figures it out, it's too late. Allen Ginsberg exclaimed while debating, and losing to, the brilliant Norman Podhoretz in 1958, "We will get you through your children!" This was not hyperbole and was the only credible point Ginsberg had made. He understood "The Plan"—and through a fit of frustration, blurted it out to the world.

There are people on both the right and the left who can achieve progressive compromise through cooperative collusion, but the first order of business is for the left to acknowledge the evils of

Woke Cultural Marxism. Unfortunately, with the Democrat Party being completely captured by violent woke ideology, that is not going to happen. Ignorance and violence drive these indoctrinated fools. Democrats started the first civil war, and please believe me, they are determined to start another.

Stop grasping at straws. Vote Republican.

WISDOM

Always revered. Rarely challenged. And for good reason. Wisdom comes from the soul, whatever that is. I've heard it described as a canon of traditions that worked, and then passed on to future generations.

What struck me when I read that is the realization that you don't have to be "smart" to be wise. But you do have to be old. Wisdom is your gut feeling, and your gut feeling is almost always right. It comes through life's experiences, both good and bad, and requires only that you keep your eyes open. A common woman or man can be, and often is, far more wise than an accomplished scholar.

These traditions or "pearls of wisdom," as they are often known, can come from the talents of a creative thinker, writer, or storyteller whose gift is to make you think and appreciate. They also come from the depth and sincerity in an elder's eyes. They are founded on the truth, the beauty, the tragedy, and the realism of the past. Therefore, the wisdom of the future can never be projected—only speculated. And nowhere in that beautiful wisdom of the future, I think, will we find Drag Queen Story Hour.

Save our kids.

Stop voting for democrats.

THE CONSEQUENCES OF

HYPOCRISY

Critical Theory: All of existing society is to be seen through the Marxist lens of oppressor vs. oppressed, combined with the concept of power dynamics through group identity, also known as identity politics. This is absolute. Therefore, no dissent can exist or be tolerated. Defining mitigating dynamics are notwithstanding. Why? Because Critical Theory says so. So, shut up.

Social Justice: The utopian result of total adherence to, and the implementation of, critical theory dogma to replace the Western civilization canon and obliterate the foundation of the enlightenment, which declares the individual as the "Ultimate Minority." (Thank you, Jordan.)

We can argue the complexities of these concepts, but at the end of the day, what you see above is what you get. The hypocrisy of the critical theorists is their intolerance of dissent as they engage in dissent. It is their way or the highway, and this is of course, in clear political terms, totalitarianism. This is fine with them as extensive Marxist literature embraces violent totalitarianism.

Both concepts ignore a multiplicity of profound and obvious factors impacting anthropological and historical development. Many of these are discussed in Dr. Thomas Sowell's book "Social Justice Fallacies." These include the geographical location and demographic makeup of people in those locations, the advantages of coastlines, and the disadvantages of mountainous regions resulting in isolation. The consequences of wars correlate with the expansion and collapse of empires. Religious adaptations (Animist vs. Abrahamic – J.D. Hill) and the availability of large animals to be exploited for agriculture and transportation also play a role. The embracing of slavery and its braking affect on economies can be demonstrated by the African continent and the American South, where the Dixies still, to this day, haven't caught up to the Yankees in the North. Sowell has even promoted the idea that some cultures are more inclined to adventure than others. Why? He admits he doesn't know but also offers the British as an example and, I will submit, the Chinese of today as another. (I can continue to ramble on, but will suggest instead to look into Dr. Sowell's work. You will not be disappointed.)

Let me suggest that the critical theorist concept of social justice, in light of what is listed above and much, much more, is notwithstanding due to its brevity and intolerance alone. At the end of the day, it's just a great big conspiracy theory. *Restricting and ignoring scholastic, logical, and empirical information is the epitome of hypocrisy.*

But social justice *is* very much alive and thriving in the minds of every woman and man who fully understand the political concepts of classical liberalism as the foundation of Western civilization. And nowhere are the most illustrative examples of those concepts than in the two founding documents of America: the Declaration of Independence and the Constitution of the United States of America. *These two documents, founded in optimism and hope, contain the brilliance and the intentions of America's Founders.* Contrast that with the nonstop ugly racism, violence, and negativity of critical theory, particularly Critical Race Theory, then make your choice.

Like the Founders, I am progressive. I'll take door number one.

HYPOCRISY AND ETYMOLOGY

Queers for Palestine? Obama's 2004 speech and Obama today? Global Cooling/Global Warming? Feminism and Title IX? ACLU and loyalty oaths vs. ACLU and diversity statements? Pronouns vs. sexual privacy? BLM racism vs. Klan racism? Red/Green Alliance? Shall I go on? Because I could for days…no? I don't blame you.

My opening paragraph sets the tone for the title of this essay. One could write a book on the consistent hypocrisy of the left over time. Rather, I would like to point to the progressive consistency of classical liberalism (conservatism) contrasted with the left.

I refuse to use the coveted moniker of "liberal" when referring to the left, as the etymology needs to change. Marxist fascism does not mix well with liberalism. Classical liberalism, as understood by enlightenment principles of Western civilization, has remained consistent for centuries: freedom and equality of the individual, capitalism, an orderly society maintained by the rule of law, steeped in logic, truth, reason, and objectivity. This is conservatism, and Conservatives are, by definition and by their embrace of Classical liberalism, Progressive Liberals.

The left embraces political opportunism and will shamelessly contradict itself for political expediency at the flip of a coin. This is neither progressive nor liberal in any sense. They engage in what I call CMCSP – Collectivism, Marxism, Communism, Socialism, Progressivism – in that order. As each "ism" failed, they would simply move on to another one. Communism: Don't you want to be part of the community? Socialism: Don't tell me you're anti-social. Progressivism: C'mon! Don't be an old boring conservative! Be progressive! Don't you know that Black Lives Matter? No one would catch on to the linguistic manipulation until they were trapped. Many would find out later that the only consistencies running through Marxist thought are hate, revenge, manipulation, and violence. CRT?... DEI?... BLM?

Times change, but hate does not. So, if hate and division are your guiding political forces, you will inevitably find yourself in a pickle as hate gets progressively marginalized through "the empathy of the West," as articulated by the intellectually astute Helen Pluckrose. This is the conundrum the Frankfurt School found itself in, which I spelled out in my previous essay, "Grasping at Straws." The hate-driven vulgar Marxism had failed, and they had to come up with a new scam: Cultural Marxism. It might have worked had they dropped the violence (which I will argue, to his credit, Gramsci tried to impose), but instead embraced Horkheimer's and Lukács' vision of Critical Theory, which gave us Critical Race Theory, both of which gave us… hate, division, and violence. The Left… so happy to be angry. This is where they dwell.

Dehumanization is always the harbinger of genocide. Nasty racist references are intentionally demonizing ("whiteness," "white privilege," "oppressor," "oppressed," to name a few) and are done through the linguistic manipulation of the left residing in the universities. This ugly name-calling is intended to achieve as much hate as possible to assist the most vile human behavior. Linguistic manipulation is the purview of the left and has enabled them to abuse political etymology. Therefore, they have an undeserved influence on political etymology. It is time for conservatives to steal their game.

Conservatives are classical liberals; hence, they are liberal progressives by any linguistic measure. Make it known.

Racism is hate, and Critical Race Theory is racism. Make it known.

Marxism is synonymous with totalitarianism. Make it known.

Capitalism gives you a reason to get out of bed in the morning. Communist socialism does not. We already knew that.

The technological advancement of alternative media (thank you, Rush) has opened a whole new world to learning, and the left is being exposed. I have held a CDL trucker's license for 45 years. There is an adage in the industry that says, "Any idiot can drive a truck." Well, as disparaging as that sounds, it's true. I would like to extrapolate that same logic to earning a doctorate in the social sciences, especially anything associated with identity studies. Yes, indeed. Any idiot can do it. This has been clearly demonstrated by the recent exposure of the Jew-hatred saturating the ivy league universities and the stunningly intellectually bereft response of the grifting leadership. The emperor has no clothes.

The Intellectual Revolution has been launched. We are no longer beholden to the elites' intellectual bullying and their sycophants in the media. Engage, debate, and when they spit in your face, as they have for the last 50 years… Spit Back!

It's the only language they know.

Class dismissed.

REPUBLICANS ARE THE

PROGRESSIVES

And have always been since 1854, when they emerged as the abolitionist force against the democrat south's institution of slavery. From Lincoln to the Radical Republicans under Thaddeus Stevens to Calvin Coolidge, Dwight Eisenhower, Richard Nixon, and Donald Trump, republicans have been, far and away, more supportive of racial equality than the Jim Crow slavers in the Democrat Party. From abolition and the fight for the 14th Amendment to the counter-revolution against woke ideology, they have always championed civil rights and true, not compromised, progressivism.

Warren Harding and the republicans fought hard and were overwhelmingly representative in passing the 19th Amendment for women's suffrage. The result was a commanding victory for Harding in 1920. Harding died in office, and his stoic vice president, Calvin Coolidge, took over the progressive republican mantle.

"Silent Cal" proved to be a dominant force for civil rights, especially the advancement of the Black population, for whom he held the highest regard. He never used bluster, hence the nickname. He did the work. (An interesting story of Cal's character: he was once confronted by a reporter who claimed he could get the president to give more than just a two-word answer to his questions. Cal's response? "You lose" — and he walked away. You don't intimidate a Vermont farmer and expect it to go well.)

Cal didn't run in '28, but we got Herbert Hoover, who was yet another republican champion of civil rights. Hoover's vice president, Charles Curtis, was Native American, and though that may come as a surprise to you, it should not, as both Hoover and Curtis were very outspoken about their disdain for racism in all its forms. The reason you are surprised is that the leftists who control education and media would never have taught you that (a practice known as "lying by omission"). They just keep up the charade that Obama was the first POC in the White House. That is not just bullshit, it is also no surprise.

Next was Franklin Roosevelt, whose record and rhetoric on civil rights vacillated according to convenience, which I submit would never have happened under Cal... or Herb. This was typical political behavior for democrats. Back then, as it is now, political expediency came first.

Then came Harry Truman, the saving grace for democrats concerning civil rights in the post-war 20th century (and a far cry from FDR) with his "Special Message to Congress on Civil Rights" in 1948. This declaration set the political and cultural tables for six decades of remarkable progressive advances for minorities, championed politically by republicans and culturally by beautiful American citizens like you and me. We saw republican icons Dwight Eisenhower and Richard Nixon guide republican majorities in Congress to pass the Civil Rights Acts of '57, '60, '64, and '68. In contrast, democrat icons JFK and RFK constantly struggled with their own party on these issues.

Then we had the political chameleon Lyndon Johnson, who, after Jack Kennedy's assassination, found it politically advantageous to sign the '64 act into law (which was a good thing) and then moved forward with his demonstrably disastrous Great Society programs (which was not). He was notoriously quoted when referencing those programs: "We'll have those niggers voting for us for the next 200 years"... a typical racist democrat with no intention of doing what is right. The lesson that should have been learned is this: whenever a democrat caresses your hand and looks sincerely into your eyes and says, "We only want to help you..." grab your wallet and run!

Then, of course, is the Democrat Big Lie, aka the Southern Strategy—Nixon's secret "dog whistle" plan (heard that before?) to flip the racist south to the GOP. Only the completely indoctrinated could fall for such nonsense. Strom Thurmond and Albert Watson alone had switched parties during the Nixon era, leaving over 200 senators, congressmen, and governors firmly ensconced with the democrats. Nixon championed the Civil Rights Act, abolishing discrimination, and pushed affirmative action through the Philadelphia Plan. Are you leftists so naïve to think that this was the behavior of a president "dog-whistling" racists? For gawd's sake, even Noam Chomsky has commented that the last liberal president we had before Obama was Richard Nixon.

The south's major push to the GOP occurred through the 80s and 90s, and the driving forces were anti-communism, patriotism, and Christian values. Sentiments had started leaning in the GOP direction in the mid-70s due to disgust with the Vietnam anti-war protesters and Obama's heroes, the Weathermen, a domestic terrorist organization. (I'm sure Bill Ayers and Barry are smiling broadly at the Tesla terror attacks as they sip their lattes together.) And here is a glaring reality: as the south became more republican, it became less racist. Chew on that.

After Nixon, we entered the disastrous Carter Administration. Although Carter's leadership failed in every governmental category, his civil rights record was solid.

But was it as solid as Nixon's? No. In the 50s and 60s, while Carter deftly played both sides of the political fence, as Democrats so often are wont to do, did Nixon do the same? No. Remember, this was the height of Jim Crow—when Blacks needed strength and conviction, which Nixon supplied, not lip service and inaction, which typified Carter.

So why is it that Nixon is always the villain and Carter always the hero? Because Nixon was a republican and Carter was a democrat. It's that simple. The early foundation of Gramsci's dream had been placed. (Please... don't bring up Watergate. This has almost no standing in this context, as the Trump-Russia collusion hoax *alone* makes Watergate look like a parking ticket.)

The next four presidents were much like Carter in the 50s and 60s —lots of virtue signaling and little substance. Despite this weak engagement, race relations improved remarkably. In 1998, 94% of Americans did not approve of interracial marriage. In 2018, 96% did. In 2009, 65 to 70% of Americans thought race relations were good and getting better. In 2019, 65 to 70% thought race relations were bad and getting worse. An exact 180 in a very short time.

So, what happened that over 100 years of steady racial progress under the mature guidance of republicans could get flipped on its head in 10? Barack Obama and Black Lives Matter. Marxism has been the soup of the day in our universities for over half a century. Barry's election was perfect timing as the elites were well aware that he, with his good looks and his silver tongue, was one of them. BLM Marxism was the violence and hate. Barry was the Fabian Marxist needed for public tolerance. Throw in the insanity of postmodern sexual wokeism and voila! The perfect political combination needed to crush Western civilization had finally arrived after "The Long March."

The hate, racism, and violence of woke cultural Marxism have ideologically captured the American Democratic Party. The biblical principles of the enlightenment—equality, reason, logic, truth, and individual rights—are the current and founding principles of the Republican Party.

Which party are the progressives? I'll take door number two, please.

DEMOCRATS VS.

REPUBLICANS

Democrats hate republicans because republicans don't agree with democrats.

Republicans hate democrats because democrats hate republicans.

These differentiating characteristics may seem trite but are quite significant, especially when coupled with leftist indoctrination, in trying to establish why we can't accept each other's attitudes. The differences in behavioral norms between the two are stark. Democrats tend to be far more angry, often at nothing of significance, than republicans. They are far more likely to break off relationships with family and friends over politics than republicans. In fact, many on the left encourage such behavior. Studies have shown that leftists are more likely to suffer from anxiety and depression than conservatives. Democrats are far more likely to see a therapist to discuss all the problems they don't really have. They spend a pile of money and leave the grifter's office smiling and feeling good about themselves. Three days later, they are right back to who they were (are) but still talking about how wonderful their therapist is. The local massage parlor would have produced the same results, and the masseuse would be far more interesting than the jerk in the sweater you just unloaded your life on. Republicans, on the other hand, are faced with trying not to hate someone who hates you for no good reason, which is a rather high bar.

The BLM demonstration riots are, to me, clear examples of this dark behavior. Without any knowledge of the facts surrounding the ostensible premise, tens of thousands of democrats poured into the streets to support rioting Antifa and BLM thugs trying to "burn it all down" - "by any means necessary." Even the slightest deviation from the CNNification of the legacy media as their source of information would have told these people that the Marxist thugs they were cheering on were completely full of shit. But they couldn't take the time because screaming in the streets with like-minded fools made them feel good about themselves. Temporarily. When the insanity cycles down, they go back to their comfortable homes and continue to be miserable. Or depressed. Or anxious. Or...

Christianity holds that hate, in all examples, is unacceptable. That is a tall order, and I admire those who adhere. However, when hating the New York Yankees because you're a Boston Red Sox fan goes from the metaphorical to the actual, we've got a problem.

ONCE

There is no global cooling, no global warming, no acid rain, no deforestation; the spotted owl is just fine, so are the polar bears, and we don't have to recycle. The Great Pacific Garbage Patch is fraudulently exaggerated to the point of assininity, major storm patterns haven't changed, and fossil fuels combined with Western colonialism have eliminated world hunger. I can go on about "never-seen-before sudden temperature spikes" nonsense and the fact that there has been zero correlation between CO2 atmospheric levels and climate mean temperature throughout the history of Earth. None of this matters to the activist woke mob who, like it or not, are running the world. The entire environmental movement has been hijacked by the Marxist Long March from noble intentions of clean air and clean water to one of the nastiest and, sadly, very effective political bullshit blizzards known to humanity. I know. I fell for it, too.

The 1970 Clean Air Act, signed into law by Richard Nixon (who?), also created the Environmental Protection Agency (arguably the most corrupt federal agency of the deep state's total corruption) and was celebrated as the solution to put us on the road to save us from—global cooling. I remember giving full-throated support and trying to convince my car-crazy buddies that we had to give up our gas-guzzling hot rods to do our part to save the planet. They thought I was falling for a crock of shit. They were right. I shook my head and walked away. I never convinced them to join me in the annual Earth Day celebrations because they knew better.

After the "Blizzard of '78," a rather sudden change in what we considered the norm in weather began to take place—it started to get warm, just like it did in the late 20s and 30s. It happened so quickly that it eliminated the man-made catastrophic global cooling crock nearly overnight. So, the lying leftists needed a brand-new lie to jam into the corrupt universities, media, and the public square. They wasted little time and quickly came up with the hysterical cry of… global warming—we're all going to die—just like global cooling. That was it for me. I apologized to my friends for having been duped by a bunch of stoned, half-drunk, know-nothing morons, and I have been fighting them ever since.

Totalitarian Marxists like (well… not like, but use) stoned, half-drunk, know-nothing morons. They understand, fully, Lenin's description of them as his "useful idiots" as they march in the streets, and so the tradition has carried on to this day. The intellectuals of Marxist thought who dominate the universities immediately understood the enormous potential of the environmental movement to help them engineer the economic collapse of Western civilization. By abusing the emotions and good intentions of decent people (you and me), they could launch an all-out war against the technologically miraculous fossil fuel industry and deliver a crippling blow to the lifeblood of—capitalism.

Copernicus was ridiculed by the elite, as was Galileo, Dr. Fred Wegener, and countless others. Why? Because the elites always hold the strings of power and are firmly ensconced with too much to lose, *even when they doubt themselves.* And who is the most curious and supportive of the great scientific minds? Those with the least to lose—the common woman and man, who are told to sit down, shut up, and do what they're told. In this regard, nothing has changed. The common woman and man are, according to the power mongers, "…the smelly Walmart people," and the elite are the self-anointed "experts" residing in their ivory towers.

They only want to help you.

When looking at the real motives of "environmentalists," Greenpeace serves as a clear example of my hypothesis. Their work in the '70s and '80s under the leadership of genuinely concerned environmentalists like Dr. Patrick Moore and others created unparalleled success in saving the whales, stopping the senseless, barbaric slaughter of baby seals, and halting nuclear bomb testing across the globe. These courageous people would literally risk their lives and were undeniably devoted to justice, not politics.

But where is Greenpeace today? Nowhere to be found other than on leftist payrolls, which is the reason the remarkable Dr. Moore is no longer with them.

Asinine, ridiculously inefficient offshore windmills are slaughtering whales.

They don't care.

Birds, especially raptors, are being decimated by strikingly ugly and inefficient land-based windmills.

They don't care.

The desert tortoise and other land mammals are being negatively impacted by millions of acres of inefficient, gawdawful ugly solar panels.

They don't care.

Hi-tech, small, safe nuclear power plants and natural gas development can reduce emissions by astronomical calculations, but are constantly obstructed by "environmentalists."

THEY DON'T FUCKING CARE!

Why? Because they have been told to sit down, shut up, and do what they're told. And that is just fine with them so long as the leftist cash keeps flowing in. As technology grows, it is doing what I said it would do 20 years ago. It is revealing that humankind is not only causing little, if any, warming to the climate; it is actually getting closer to my prediction that technology will eventually prove that, other than the Heat Island Effect, we have nothing to do with it whatsoever. Zero. Zip. Natha. The Earth is not flat! Once the Marxist thugs are in control, the entire environmental movement will get the fascist boot out the door. Why? Because they know their fucked-up economy doesn't stand a chance without fossil fuels. Greenpeace will become the Third Reich.

So, where does all of this leave us? In an ideological footrace with the woke Marxist thugs for the future of humanity. They will employ any farce—from pictures of starving polar bears to dim-witted celebrities (think Leonardo DiCaprio and Jesse Smollett) to crush Western civilization. Time is of the essence, and they know it. They must pull off the results of their blizzard of bullshit—which is totalitarian power—before we can do anything about it. I fell for it once.

Once.

ABSTRACTIONS

Imagine, just for fun, that the Jew-hating, racist, misogynistic, misanthropic, totalitarian, homophobic, genocidal maniac, Che Guevara, had decided on a strategy of becoming a U.S. citizen to undermine the West from within (an option chosen by leftists much smarter than he) instead of armed revolution. Upon taking residence in the USA, his first order of business would be to run for political office as a democrat. In the '60s, he would not have won at a higher level of political prominence (which, admittedly, would have been his style) but at a lower level—say, mayor of a small town—he may have.

Now let's move this imaginary scene to our more contemporary political landscape. Let's choose 2010 to 2024…ish. Here he could run for that higher position, again as a democrat, and probably win in a landslide. One needs only to tally his t-shirt sales in cities like Los Angeles, San Francisco, Portland, and New York to confirm.

My point is this: Gramsci's Long March Through the Institutions, as articulated by his devoted student Rudy Dutschke, has *firmly* established its roots. These are dark times for humanity. The universities, Gramsci's primary target, have become the enemy of the people. Reform is not an option, as the maniacal left knows no compromise. The 100,000,000 corpses of the 20th century may be matched by 21st-century fanatical woke intolerance. They really want to kill us. Just listen to their cultural heroes: Noam Chomsky and his intellectually pathetic views on the "unvaccinated"; Noel Ignatiev and his call for abolishing the white race; Donald Moss declaring that being white is a mental disorder; or consider that over half of democrats approve of assassinating Trump and Musk. And then, of course, Luigi. All of these thugs are enthusiastically embraced by the left. If from there you come away with anything other than the woke culture of violence espousing eliminationist rhetoric, then you don't understand the basic concepts of eliminationist rhetoric. *Only indoctrination can produce this level of depravity.* Thank the ivy league.

John Dewey, the "Father of American Education," said in 1951, "Give us two generations in control (of education) and we will control everything." Even Mr. Dewey (a leftist, of course) could not have imagined the consequences of his language in the mid-20th century, as he was not, by any analysis, a totalitarian.

But times have changed. We must collapse the educational structure immediately and return to the principles of Classical Liberalism now… before it is too late.

"Never again" may be right around the corner should the Marxist Guevarians regain the political upper hand. Don't let it happen. Stop voting for democrats.

DECISIONS, DECISIONS

Independent voters, in their "I'm so much smarter than you" smugness, often find themselves unable to choose a side to vote for because of their self-anointed ability to "see through the bullshit" on both sides—or their inability to put down the remote and pick up a book.

Well, I have a solution. Vote for the side that doesn't want to kill you if you don't vote for them.

Vote Republican.

Gleichschaltung

English translation: synchronization. This was Nazi vernacular for their program that mirrors, and indeed, I will argue below, inspires what we call today—Cancel Culture.

Let me first say that the evil is obvious at first blush with the affiliations of both: Synchronization = Nazi, and Cancel Culture = Woke. Politically, they are functionally the same.

Synchronization policy of the National Socialist Party: Saturate all German institutions—education, media, corporations, banks, government agencies, military, civic organizations, entertainment and sports, all cultural venues, virtually the entirety of both governmental and private life—with absolute adherence to Nazi dogma. Anyone speaking any criticism of the regime is to be immediately humiliated, fired, reputationally rejected from society, and/or jailed. Or worse.

Cancel Culture of the woke Marxist totalitarians: ditto. (The "worse" is on the way.)

"Mygawd!", you say. "There are no totalitarians in America!"

Buckle up.

Zack DePiero, an English professor and a champion of working with disadvantaged youth, particularly minorities, was excited to land a teaching position at Penn State. Unfortunately, his enthusiasm was short-lived as the bright, articulate, and accomplished scholar quickly ran headlong into the demonstrably totalitarian DEI ethos at the university. His reticence to grade students based on their race drew the wrath of the administrators, supervisors, and "scholars" throughout the school. He was summoned to the office of affirmative action and informed that "There is a problem with the white race" and "White teachers are the problem," and was strongly advised to attend anti-racist workshops, "Until you get it." He was told that if his students didn't score evenly across racial lines, he would be condemned as a racist. An "antiracist scholar" (grifter) giving these workshops drew a correlation between "promoting white English" and "killing people of color," and claimed that racism against Whites is acceptable and that it is not possible to be racist against White people. (Yes, the glaring contradiction is obvious. This kind of asinine claptrap is what passes for intellectual discourse in today's universities.) The continuous barrage of anti-white, hillbilly racism is simply too much to list. But please understand what these brainwashed intellectual totalitarians put this honorable man through was pure hell. He got canceled.

A six-year-old (A SIX-YEAR-OLD!) biracial boy in the public school system in Bellevue, Washington, was told to "choose" his race. His mother found out. When she started to look into the situation, she quickly discovered the reason her little boy was singled out for this disgusting nonsense. She and her husband are both vocal supporters of Trump. She sued and won.

Tabia Lee, a delightful Black woman, is a serious multiculturalist with a PhD in Education Leadership and Administration. She landed a position as the Faculty Director for the Office of Equity, Social Justice, and Multicultural Education (covers it all, does it not?) at DeAnza College in Cupertino, California. Shortly after arriving, she suggested in a meeting that they use a Google doc to help organize different initiatives and agendas to efficiently utilize their time. She was immediately attacked by her colleagues with charges of "white-speaking," "whitesplaining," and "white supremacy" because organizing, efficiency, and timing were all tenets of "whiteness." (Whiteness—my gawd, what a disgusting, hate-filled, hillbilly- backward, racist word!) The harassment and bullying lunacy she faced from all levels was stunning. Later, she suggested that Jewish students be included in a list of students to be protected from harassment on campus. In a conversation with her supervising dean, she was told that Jews are white oppressors and that her department needed to focus on de-centering whiteness. The Jews never made the list. The only list they are eligible for in today's education hierarchy is Schindler's.

Ilya Shapiro, a well-respected scholar, was suspended from Georgetown Law for criticizing Biden for declaring he would only choose a Black woman for the Supreme Court. Shapiro's argument was that eligible Black women made up just under 3% of the available candidates, and therefore, using this prerequisite effectively made it impossible to select the most qualified person for the Court. Look at who we got. Obviously, he was right. He got canceled.

A Michigan community college had students arrested for distributing copies of The Constitution on Constitution Day. Do you think they arrested anyone for distributing BLM propaganda on any day at all? You're right. Neither do I.

Bruce Gilley, a man with more balls than any matador in all of Spain, had two of his works canceled by the woke thugs. The journal that was about to publish one received legitimate death threats (from the party of violence, I'm sure) to its staff. So, Gilley, unlike his leftist critics confronted with the same situation, withdrew the piece. (The implicit accusation is mine, not Mr. Gilley's.) The other, a biography of a prominent British colonialist, was canceled by the publisher after a radical leftist from Toronto declared it offensive. A gentleman (yes, a gentleman in the late 20th century context—we can discuss that later here at Billerica U) wrote a widely circulated letter to the publisher declaring he was sick and tired of White people regulating what people of color in Southeast Asia and the African continent can or cannot read. Indeed, the hypocrisy is glaring. He makes a rock-solid argument that the woke actually epitomize white supremacy while masquerading as liberators. Rush said it 30 years ago: "If you want to know what the left is guilty of, just look at what they are accusing you of." You bet, Rush. No college degree required.

These examples are a fraction of a fraction of the countless atrocities (yes, intellectual atrocities) against the non-woke, not just in the corrupt halls of the universities, but in the K-12 curriculum as well. The entire "system" these thugs want to tear down is already *saturated* by their sycophants, who are there to tear it down. Throughout every university, faculty and students are required to announce their pronouns and gender identity, and don't you *dare* resist. If you do, you fail. You're a "straight A student?" Well, not anymore. Get in line or get out!

The era of McCarthyism saw 13% of academics afraid of voicing their opinions for fear of retaliation. In 2022, during the era of the toxic woke, that rate was 40% and climbing.

The number of professors who have been terminated for refusing to adhere to woke exceeds the number of professors who refused to cower to McCarthyism by a factor of 10.

In 2010, there were 20 attempts to punish professors for using free speech. From 2014 to 2023, there were over 1,000, two-thirds of which were successful. Hello? ACLU? Anybody home?

80% of college students today censor themselves to avoid cancellation or humiliation.

82% of Americans think cancel culture is a problem.

A Texas college fired faculty for criticizing Biden's covid policy. They were fired for being right.

90% of today's universities restrict free speech through "speech codes." If you think these codes are not egregiously going beyond the standard of "shouting fire in a theater," I'm sorry, you're a fool.

Herbert Marcuse was a big fan of synchronization/cancel culture. As to be expected from Herb, he came up with his own twisted title for the exact same practice: "Repressive Tolerance." That kind of linguistic manipulation scares you and me. The left sees it as a healthy necessity.

Even Taylor Swift has rather articulately voiced her concern on the issue. (Though I appreciate your input, Ms. Swift, it seems contradictory to endorse Kamala, who clearly is not on your intellectual level. Perhaps we could delve into this dichotomy over a cocktail at your place of choosing. Yes, I'm asking you out.)

If you think we're "out of the woods" because Trump (God bless him) got elected, you better think again. This fight is going the full 12 rounds, and they just lost round 4. They don't quit; they just change the sign on the door. They'll come out of that corner like Mike Tyson, and we better be ready.

Gleichschaltung is Cancel Culture. We are living in Berlin, 1935, and we are headed to Moscow, 1952. From Hollywood to media to education to the corporate boardrooms, "Never Again" is, once again, raising its ugly, racist head. Wake up to woke—NOW! Before the left slaughters another 100 million souls the same way Iron Mike crushed his opponents when they flinched.

OBSERVATIONS

JFK: Ask not what your country can do for you; ask what you can do for your country.

Woke: If you're White, don't ask anything. Sit down, shut up, and do what we say. If you're not White, you may speak only if we approve of what you have to say. If we don't; sit down, shut up, and do what we say.

As I said in my previous essay, we are living in Berlin, 1935; we are headed to Moscow, 1952. This is not creative hyperbole. Western civilization is being swamped from the left by the Lysenkoist ethos that says White people suck, men can have babies, and fuck the Jews. The ubiquitous and often repeated post-WW2 declaration to the world, "Never Again," has lost its significance. In fact, I have noticed that since the explosion of woke ideology, it is hardly ever heard. The intensity of contemporary Jew-hatred has not been seen since Nazi Germany, likewise the intensity of intolerance within woke ideology. This is not a coincidence.

A remarkable number of people were shocked—"SHOCKED!"—at the explosion of Jew-hate across Western universities *immediately* following 10/7. I was not, and neither were the common woman and man. I was, however, somewhat surprised at the level of ignorance and stupidity of all those people who were —"SHOCKED!" Most of them are graduates, students, or supporters of these leftist institutions, and yet, somehow, they are at a loss for an explanation. They are so blind to their indoctrination and their role in "The Long March" that they are clueless about the Jew-hating BDS movement championed by Students for Justice in Palestine, CAIR, an endless stream of "non-profits," a plethora of prominent democrats, and nearly all of the universities. Most of them would stare blankly if you mentioned Gramsci's strategy and his influence, along with Horkheimer's Critical Theory, to the foundational principles of the Frankfurt School from which the evil ideology of woke evolved, in which anti-semitism, by way of colonialism, is firmly ensconced.

Woke. There's that ugly word again. In this 10/7 iteration, we see the ostensibly liberal left joining forces within a red/green alliance with any Jew-hating entity, left or right, throughout the Global

Intifada, and it is always the same: hate, violence, and just a remarkable blend of ignorance and stupidity fully endorsed by the universities and the Democrat Party. Woke is how democrats "strive" to "bring people together." My mother had the perfect "pearl of wisdom" for these self-centered collegiates: "Stupid with knowledge." It took a long time for me to understand the profundity of that statement, but today… I do. Thanks, Mom.

Decent people instinctively know that "woke" is wrong. It doesn't take an ivy league degree to understand that it is founded on hate. In fact, if you have a college degree, you may never be able to figure that out. The common woman and man are constantly trying to figure out a clear-cut definition of woke, which is kept purposely vague by design—vagueness fosters confusion that helps destabilize societies.

So, Dear Reader, please refer to my comprehensive, concise, and brilliant definition in my second essay, "What is Woke?" for a clear-eyed view of what, exactly, is going on. For the sake of brevity, you can slug your coffee, understand what we're facing, and get on with your day, which is busy because you're conservative (whether you know it or not) and have a job.

The woke could not care less for all the causes they ostensibly care about other than using them as tools "to deconstruct, dismantle, and replace the entire system." (That is Marxist DEI language, not mine.) In other words, the total destruction of Western civilization… by any means necessary. Once this is accomplished, the cultural Marxists will kick much of woke out the door as quickly as they invited it in for two reasons. First, a totalitarian society can't function without the hated hierarchy they just destroyed. Second, the left will always eat its own for political expediency. Nobody likes woke.

Learn it, fight it, stop it. Or, please believe me… your children will pay.

THE FALLACY OF EQUITY

If equity were possible (which, of course, it is not), then within a generation or so of its initial implementation, we would all be insane. The first consideration is that it would require absolute adherence to Totalitarian Cultural Marxism and its obliteration of capitalism, "whiteness"- (private property), and freedom. As this vile and racist ideology metastasizes throughout society, the psychological toll on human capital would grow exponentially. (Think covid lockdowns—cancel culture.)

With everyone the same, there would be nothing. No reason to laugh or cry. No reason to love. No regret. No anticipation. No appreciation… no fear. No concern. No pride. No sense of accomplishment… no lessons learned. No beauty—no nothing.

To be human would be a waste of time. I think that is exactly what the woke Marxists want—with them in charge.

Of course.

IT DOESN'T MATTER

Is there a Heaven?

Maybe.

Is there a "God"?

I don't know.

Will your conscience live on in spirituality after you die?

It doesn't matter.

Western civilization has done more to improve the human condition than all other civilizations combined, and in a remarkably (yes, Miraculously) short period of time. It was founded on the solid worldview principles of Christianity. Therefore, Christianity is, logically to me, the way forward. The way forward is to improve what you left behind. This is the goal of the lessons taught in the Bible.

So, am I a Christian?

Well… I guess so.

Was Jesus Christ the Son of God?

It doesn't matter.

SOMETIMES

Sometimes things are simpler than they seem. Sometimes they really are quite complicated, like in STEM. But when it comes to the "Great Thinkers" of philosophy – Confucius, Aristotle, Kant, Hegel, Marx, Nietzsche, et al., I think we've been had.

Reading them is fun. Reading them can be thought-provoking. But reading them can also be a waste of time because most of what they have to say has long been settled by the wisdom of the common woman and man, which determines the psychological destiny of humankind. (Arguably, Hegel and his dialectic of science, spirituality, and reason, and contemporary Sowell, with his idea of Consequential Knowledge rooted in the wisdom of the common woman and man, were the only ones who may have gotten it right. We'll have to save that discussion for a more in-depth study at Billerica U.)

So, let's take some examples of my hypothesis. Let's start with woke. The philosophical tenets of woke pull from Marx, Gramsci, critical theory, and postmodernism. These thinkers and theories combined bring on a tsunami of deep philosophical considerations blended with a dizzying barrage of bullshit. But the common woman and man have long ago settled their competing arguments: the idea of trying to crush Jesus Christ, Shakespeare, Johann Pachelbel, and Dr. Martin Luther King really sucks. Straight up.

Another—Queer Theory. Here we have what seems to be deep and profound descriptions of sexual reality outside the accepted norms of a functioning society. The mostly fringe behavior has some people examining themselves and their own sexuality and joining the irrational party. The added numbers (acceptance) embolden the argument while disregarding the still insignificant number of adherents. Queer theorists dismiss this and two other prominent factors. One: the common woman and man instinctively understand that parameters must be established for societal survival. Two: the common woman and man are not narcissistic twits who only care about their own desires. They actually care about a functioning society. Why? Because they have kids. They fully understand that pedophilia and incest are fucked up. Michel Foucault and Judith Butler, in all their "brilliance," simply can't figure out the basics of humanistic cooperation for the survival of society. Even if they could, they wouldn't care, as they would never allow the health of society to stand in the way of their intellectual narcissism. They would have too much to lose. In spite of their brilliant bluster, they are, in fact, shallow as a mud puddle.

We could go into more, but I think, at this point, my point has been made. The common woman and man instinctively evolve deterministically for the greater good. Most conflagrations of humanity occur when the "Great Thinkers" get in the way.

THE 180

I often use, as do other political junkies like myself, The 180 as an argumentative tool. The 180 generally involves taking a quote or position from your opponent and flipping (180 degrees) the participants in the exercise to establish hypocrisy. This style of discourse can be very effective. It can also blow up in your face, so I suggest using it judiciously. It is usually employed in discussions of various contemporary topics on a micro level and often in a drunken stupor. Here, I would like to ramp up The 180 to the macro level and then ask you, Dear Reader, to give long contemplation to my hypothesis before either agreeing or flipping out and calling me the social media-type names of which we are both guilty. Let us begin.

As we have learned from Dr. Sowell in Social Justice Fallacies, the European continent was probably the most ideally globally located continent for trade, commerce, and economic growth in the world. Those geographical advantages and other anthropological and historical events, not the least of which was Charles Martel's victory at the Battle of Tours in 732 CE, all combined to make Europe the wealthiest region in the world. With wealth comes literacy. With literacy comes education. With wealth, literacy, and education comes adventure and expansion, resulting in powerful empires. So, the question is: what do empires do with that power to move humanity in a progressive trajectory toward the good? Some do nothing but enslave and plunder. Think Aksum and Aztec. Others try to progress humanity as they expand. Think of the Mongols (believe it or not) and others, such as Islam. But none throughout history and the anthropological progress of humankind has done more than Western civilization to improve life on this planet. It's not even close. There is no argument. The jungle is wet, the Sonoran Desert is not, and you're not a two-spirited dipshit.

So… what if… what if, for an intellectual thought exercise, we assume that the European continent was inhabited by people with black skin and the African continent, along with the southern hemisphere, was inhabited by people with white skin? What would be different in the world today? Nothing. The wealthier would be Black, and the less wealthy would be White. That's it. Any other conclusion is racist. Period.

Human nature is consistent and controlled by a Power far greater than us. No amount of social engineering will change it.

Gobblesh The 180!

CONCLUSION: ALL BY DESIGN

I read "None Dare Call It Treason" by John Stormer in 1974. I started listening to Rush around 1985 because my '72 Oldsmobile radio only had AM. When parents were baffled by schools not keeping score of their kids' sporting events by '88–90ish, I was not. When I explained to them that this was the radical left trying to undermine our culture, many of them would laugh. They're not laughing anymore.

As the insidious "Long March" makes its way through our institutions, millions of people scratch their heads and wonder aloud, "What the hell is wrong with these people?" My answer is the same as Michael Corleone's to the Nevada senator in Godfather II… "Nothing."

It is All by Design.

They want to be seen as unreasonable, as it serves contemporary Marxist ideology in a myriad of ways. The first and foremost is that it gets everyday folks like you and me arguing with each other over nonsense. The more nonsensical the better. Hence; "Woke." This fosters division, which is essential to destabilizing society to initiate collapse. This is the driving force of the woke left's embrace of the lunacy of postmodernism that says there is no truth, no reason, no logic, no reality. That the firmly established scientific fact that there are only two sexes is merely a social construct. (And they call us "science deniers.") That there is an infinite number of genders and identities. Today, you're a man. Tomorrow, a woman. Friday morning, you're non-binary. Friday afternoon, you're a '62 Studebaker.

The pronoun debate is presented as a non-problem, and that would be reasonable if they were not coming after your kids or trying to legislate it into law as compelled speech. The fact that they are is alarming for obvious reasons. This is why a Canadian man was imprisoned for refusing to use his brainwashed daughter's pronouns. You better make sure you're not committing a microaggression by asking innocuous questions to the intellectually stunted woke fanatic, like—Where are you from?—or—Where do you work? It will be deemed offensive, and no apology will be accepted—so don't bother. You'll be prosecuted anyway. Or, at our current stage in the U.S., at least canceled. If you think the American left isn't *fully devoted* to achieving the insanity of the Canadian left and beyond… you're dreaming. Wake up!

What appears to be insane to the sane is actually not insane at all. It is the carefully considered potential results of the Marxists embracing strange bedfellows such as the postmodernists and radical Islam as a means to get to where they want to go—totalitarianism. Once there, the postmodernists and the Islamists will get the fascist boot out the door. Do you really think Marx, Engels, and Gramsci were stupid enough to believe gender ideology or a worldwide Islamic Caliphate would be a good thing? Please.

The left knows that Western civilization is on the right path for humanity. They're not stupid. They fully understand that their quest for Marxist utopia is unattainable, especially when success rates of both these ideologies are stacked up against each other. Only a fool would think otherwise, and they are not fools. So, what has driven this insanity for over 175 years? The answer is threefold. First; *power.* Second; elitists controlling the universities are intellectual narcissistic twits who will *never* admit when they are wrong. Third; the initial indoctrinating principle they use in those universities is—HATE—the most powerful political tool. Everything else flows from there.

Their proletariat vs. bourgeois materialist revolution had failed, and so their heirs had to come up with a new strategy, *no matter how bizarre.* Desperation will make intellectual narcissists throw spaghetti against the wall. Christianity is slammed at every opportunity, and Islam is a religion of peace. Men are toxic, and drag queens are awesome, especially when they are reading stories to your children. And don't you dare ask the obvious, or you will be labeled as a hate-mongering white supremacist, whether you're White or not. Never mind that people of color don't want these ruthless fucking lunatics near their kids either. Is that offensive to you? Well, guess what? The Sisters of Perpetual Indulgence are offensive to me. So, fuck off.

If you look at what appears to be nonsense from the perspective of a ruthless political strategy to cripple Western Civilization (caps intended), it all makes sense. And if education, the prominent methodology, can be captured while responsible society is at work, it's actually brilliant.

Laugh no more. It is… All by Design.

THE END

~~~
~~~

THE GULL

The stillness of the morning awakens and delights my senses. Only now, while the world sleeps, is the time right for a truly heartfelt song. The coffee, prepared by the evening servant, has a hidden bitterness, though it is perfectly brewed. I hoist the cup and pass through my excessive home out to the sun-drenched deck as a tinge of guilt bites at my soul.

Out of the northeast skies approaches the majestic gull, his wings spread in controlled and effortless flight. The grace and beauty of his landing induce a special thrill in me. A thrill so special, in fact, that I shroud its affect in secrecy so that even he is unaware of my joy.

We routinely exchange our greetings as he nonchalantly walks toward the morsel of bread on the rail that I have placed for him to dine.

"Good morning, My Friend."

"Good morning, Fool," he quietly replies.

"My Friend" is the name I have chosen for him, as he is the only one whose candid honesty deserves the title. "Fool" is the name he has chosen for me in honor of that same candid honesty. I accept the title and take no offense, as none is intended. For in my daily struggle with the truth, we both know it is appropriate.

"Where do your travels take you today?" I ask as he slowly and deliberately consumes his bread.

"Today I will fly south and out to sea to lunch and spend the day with a fisherman who sings a lively song. He may seem strange to you, as he has nothing aside from his small vessel and his happiness. Ah, but I must go now, for it is a long flight."

He crouches on his perch and begins the spread of his wings in preparation of flight. The flowing spring into the air once again induces the special and secret thrill that fills my heart.

"Goodbye, Fool," is his farewell bid as he flies away.

"Goodbye, My Friend," is mine. Who is this fisherman? I wonder.

"Wait, My Friend!" I shout into the trail of the bird's flight. "What is your name for the fisherman?"

The great bird glances back over his wing.

"Content," he replies. I pause only for a moment.

"And his name for you?" I ask at the top of my voice as the distance grows rapidly between us. He does not immediately respond, but after some hesitation, begins a long, circular trajectory back to my stance. He approaches me swiftly and cocks his head in my direction so that our eyes meet for the first time as he passes within my grasp.

"My Friend" is his final and unemotional answer.

And as I watch him in distant flight, the day's first smile slowly reaches my soul.

Bruce O'Brien